By:
Laurie Leader

Illustrated by:
Amber Russell

Copyright © 2021 by Laurie Leader

All rights reserved. No part of this publication may be reproduced, distributed, or transmitted in any form or by any means, including photocopying, recording, or other electronic or mechanical methods, without the prior written permission of the author/publisher. For permission requests, please contact the author.

Hardback ISBN: 979-8-9891445-0-1

Paperback ISBN: 979-8-9891445-1-8

A birthday wish come true,
Alli squealed with such glee
Her kitten had arrived.
She was happy as could be!

A plush bundle o' fur
With orange, white and black
Like Halloween colors,
Her own calico cat!

Hand-picked from the litter
And given a sweet name.
"Mandy's what I'll call her!"
Alli proudly exclaimed.

Life was grand for Mandy

And Alli felt the same.

They did everything together

But things were 'bout to change.

One day, Alli came home—
A creature in her arms—
A blob of matted fur.
Mandy was quite alarmed.

This mass of nastiness
Was none other than a cat
Saved from dumpster living
And smelling like a rat.

Angry and now itchy,
Mandy began to scratch;
fleas were jumping off Zig
And landing on HER back!

In that very moment Mandy received worse news. She heard those awful words: "BATH time for BOTH of you!"

The horror of it all! Mandy was not inclined.

Into the tub she went
With Big Zig right behind.

With Zig's unwelcome entry
Mandy's world forever changed.
She would have to share all things.
Oh, what a crying shame!

TODAY

S-T-R-E-T-C-H

Letting out a loud cry,
Mandy's ready to eat!
fish 'n bits have arrived.
What a flavorful treat!

Mandy plods to her box for a quick potty break. She then spots a big gift Zig has left in his wake.

"Hrumph....how rude of that Zig! I'll show him!" Mandy squawks. "It's time he learns the truth— That it's ME who is boss!"

Tired from the excitement,
Mandy's ready to plop.
She starts looking around
for a warm, sunny spot.

She yawns and she stretches,
Drifting off to dreamland
Where she begins scheming
About all her big plans.

S-C-R-E-E-T-C-H!
BEEP BEEP!

Awake, Mandy wonders,
"What's that noise that I hear?
Ahhh...the bus has arrived!
My girl Alli is here!"

Smiling, Alli skips in
And gives Mandy a hug.

Then she swoops Big Zig up
In her arms for some love.

"How I've missed my sweet cats!"
Alli tenderly contends.
"These are my babies and
My favorite fur friends!"

Later, Alli plops down
In the big easy chair,
And each kitty hops up;
In her lap they both share.

But for a brief moment
They are such a cute pair!

Mandy is rejoicing—
Sweet victory declared!

Not to worry, my dears,
Zig reclaims his own space
With a slobbery kiss
Upon Mandy's mad face!

"This should be a lesson!"
Alli firmly proclaims.
Mandy feels contrite now,
Bowing her head in shame.

She daintily reaches out
And touches Big Zig's paw,
Then whispers, "I'm sorry
for causing you to fall."

Zig is so delighted
By Mandy's sweet amends.
He has always wanted
To be forever friends!

The moral here is clear:
follow the Golden Rule.
Treat others with kindness;
There's no need to be cruel.

Lastly, remember this:
Always strive to do right,
And cherish great friendships
for they make the world bright!

Real-Life Inspirations

Alli with her friend Jonathan (author's son).

Alli in dance attire.

Mandy begging for food.